The American Mosaic
Immigration Today

First-Generation Americans

Sara Howell

PowerKiDS press.

New York

Published in 2015 by The Rosen Publishing Group, Inc.
29 East 21st Street, New York, NY 10010

Copyright © 2015 by The Rosen Publishing Group, Inc.

First Edition

Editors: Jennifer Way and Norman D. Graubart
Book Design: Andrew Povolny
Photo Research: Katie Stryker

Photo Credits: Cover Kali9/E+/Getty Images; p. 4 Donald R. Swartz/
Shutterstock.com; p. 5 Andy Dean Photography/Shutterstock.com; p. 6
Dan Thornberg/Shutterstock.com; p. 7 Orham Cam/Shutterstock.com;
p. 8 Andrey Bayda/Shutterstock.com; p. 9 Steven Frame/Shutterstock.
com; p. 10 Pablo Calvog/Shutterstock.com; p. 11 Andrew Burton/Getty
Images; p. 13 Mike Watson Images/Moodboard/Thinkstock;
p. 14 John Moore/Getty Images; p. 15 Feverpitched/iStock/Thinkstock;
p. 17 Comstock Images/Stockbyte/Getty Images; p. 18 Monkey Business
Images/Shutterstock.com; p. 19 Kamira/Shutterstock.com;
p. 20 Jupiterimages/Digital Vision/Getty Images; p. 21 Sergey Novikov/
Shutterstock.com; p. 22 Andrea Pistolesi/The Image Bank/Getty Images.

Library of Congress Cataloging-in-Publication Data

Howell, Sara.
First-generation Americans / by Sara Howell. — First Edition.
    pages cm. — (The American mosaic : immigration today)
Includes index.
ISBN 978-1-4777-6747-4 (library binding) — ISBN 978-1-4777-6748-1
(pbk.) — ISBN 978-1-4777-6651-4 (6-pack)
1. Immigrants—United States—Juvenile literature. 2. United States—
Emigration and immigration—Juvenile literature. I. Title.
E184.A1H68 2015
305.9'069120973—dc23
                                        2014003065

Manufactured in the United States of America

CPSIA Compliance Information: Batch #WS14PK1: For Further Information contact Rosen
Publishing, New York, New York at 1-800-237-9932

Contents

From Immigrant to Citizen

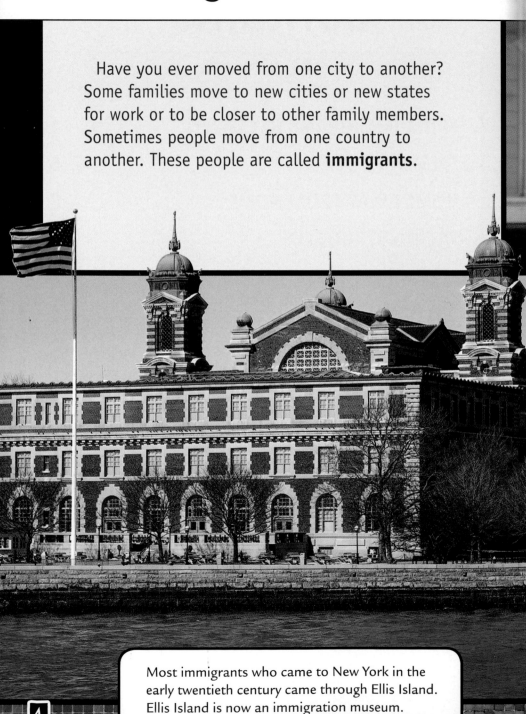

Have you ever moved from one city to another? Some families move to new cities or new states for work or to be closer to other family members. Sometimes people move from one country to another. These people are called **immigrants**.

Most immigrants who came to New York in the early twentieth century came through Ellis Island. Ellis Island is now an immigration museum.

First-generation American families live all over the United States. They may be your next-door neighbors!

Many immigrants who move to the United States choose to become **citizens**. Immigrants who become citizens are often called first-generation Americans. Sometimes the term "first-generation American" is used to describe a child born in the United States to immigrant parents. This book uses the term to mean an immigrant who moves to the United States and becomes a US citizen.

Citizens by Law

The Fourteenth Amendment to the Constitution states that all people born in the United States are citizens.

There are two ways to become a citizen of the United States. The first is to be born here. These people are called **natural-born citizens**. The second is to become a citizen by law. This is called **naturalization**.

Becoming a naturalized citizen is hard. Immigrants must live in the United States for a certain number of years. They must show that they can read, speak, and write English and that they understand how the US government works. Though it is not easy, people choose to become naturalized citizens because they want to enjoy the rights of American citizens.

The American system of government can be hard to understand. Still, you must know how it works to pass a citizenship test.

Home Away from Home

Often, new immigrants will choose to settle in neighborhoods where others from their home country have settled. This leads to areas with large numbers of immigrants from the same country. For example, the Albany Park neighborhood of Chicago is nicknamed Koreatown for its large Korean **population**. The city of Miami, Florida, has a neighborhood called Little Havana, where many Cuban immigrants have settled.

This is a street in Chinatown, a neighborhood in San Francisco.

NO SMOKING IN THIS AREA

NO FUMAR EN ESTA ÁREA

This sign says the same thing in English and Spanish. Some places have signs like these so immigrants who are still learning English can read them.

In these immigrant communities, first-generation Americans often use their native language. There are television programs and newspapers available in the native language, too. Members of the community can come together to celebrate cultural activities, such as festivals and holidays.

Facing Struggles

First-generation Americans often face many struggles. Some come to the United States with a good education and many important skills. However, many arrive with very little education and few useful skills. This can make it difficult to find jobs and earn money. Some first-generation Americans try to earn enough money to support themselves as well as family members back in their home countries.

One way to immigrate to America is to be hired by an American business.

Shaun Donovan is the US secretary of housing and urban development. His office deals with housing issues, such as landlord discrimination.

Finding a place to live can also be difficult. First-generation Americans who try to rent homes sometimes face **discrimination** from landlords. Buying a home can also be hard for someone whose first language is not English.

Learning the Language

Many new immigrants speak little or no English when they arrive in the United States. To become naturalized citizens, they must learn to read, write, and speak basic English. However, it can take new citizens many more years to become **fluent**, or able to use a language easily and correctly.

Communities with many immigrants often have **resources** available to help people learn and practice English. English as a second language, or ESL, classes may be offered at libraries, community colleges, or community centers. ESL classes may also be offered to students in public schools.

There are computer programs that teach English, too.

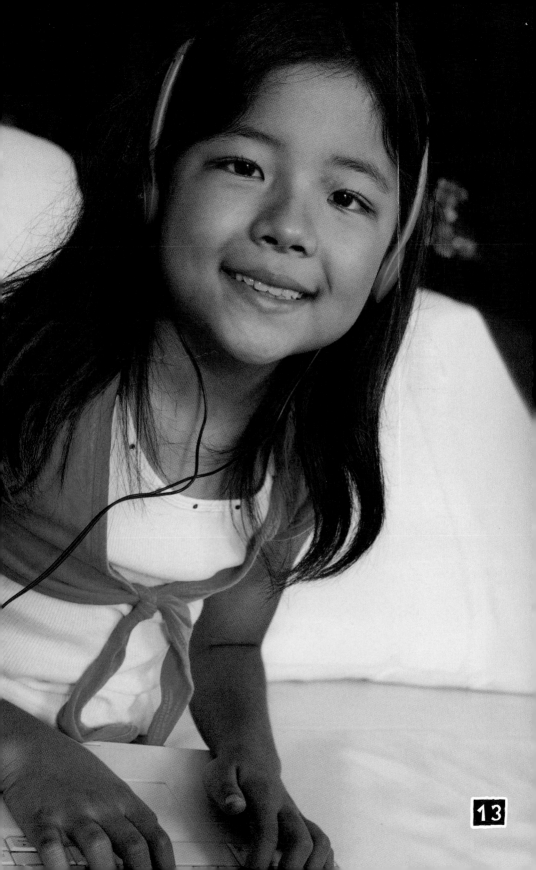

Culture Clash

This is the Three Kings Day parade in New York. Many Hispanic immigrants celebrate this Christian holiday on January 6th.

Many first-generation Americans come from **cultures** very different from that of the United States. Culture is the beliefs, practices, and arts of a group of people. First-generation Americans are often used to different foods and clothing, as well as different values and traditions.

It can take time to get used to living in a new culture. There may be times when cultural practices cause misunderstandings and hurt feelings. For example, in Japan, people show respect by lowering their eyes and not making eye contact. A student from Japan may get in trouble at school for not looking his teacher in the eye in the United States.

Making new friends as a first-generation American can be hard. Sports can bring you and your classmates together, though.

Melting and Mixing

First-generation Americans try to balance their home cultures and their new American **identities**. Some people think of the United States as a melting pot. Each culture is absorbed by, or mixed into, American culture. This idea is called **assimilation**.

Others choose to see the United States more as a salad bowl. The pieces of the salad, such as the lettuce, tomatoes, and olives, are different. Together, they create the salad. With this idea, immigrants keep many parts of their culture. Those pieces then come together to create our ever-changing American culture.

This Hispanic immigrant family is celebrating July 4th with a picnic. This is an example of how cultures mix in America.

Parents and Kids

In the United States today, one in every four children is the child of immigrant parents. These children are often called second-generation Americans. Because they were born in the United States, they are US citizens at birth.

In some immigrant families, not all children are natural-born citizens. Only those born in the United States are born with American citizenship.

If your parents don't speak English well, they may not be able to help you with your homework. This can be a problem for first-generation American kids.

The children of immigrants sometimes feel pushed by their parents to do very well in school and work extra hard. Children may be more concerned, though, with fitting in. It can also be hard for kids when their parents are not fluent in English. Their parents may not be able to help with homework or get them help at school with any special needs.

The 1.5 Generation

Some immigrants are very young when they arrive in the United States. They were born in a **foreign** country, so they are first-generation Americans, like their parents. However, these kids have grown up in the United States from a very early age. This means they often have more in common with second-generation kids. These kids are sometimes called the 1.5 generation.

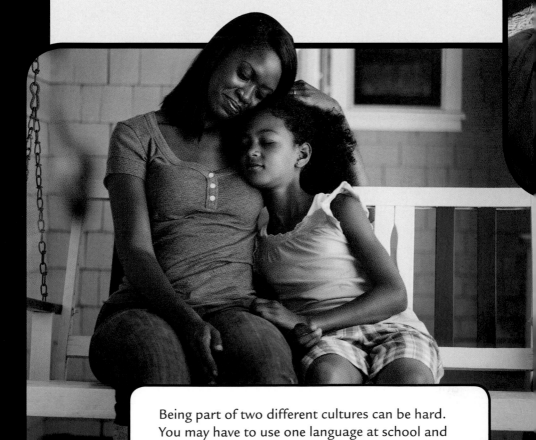

Being part of two different cultures can be hard. You may have to use one language at school and a different one at home.

You may meet other kids in your school who come from immigrant families. Talk to them about what it's like to be a first-generation American.

Members of the 1.5 generation can sometimes feel like they do not fully belong to either culture. They may speak English fluently and feel comfortable with American culture. However, they may also have memories of their home country and their family's journey toward citizenship.

The American Mosaic

The melting pot and the salad bowl are both great ways of thinking about American culture. You can also think of American culture as a **mosaic.** A mosaic is a larger picture made by fitting many small pieces together.

Each person who lives in the United States, whether immigrant or natural-born citizen, is a piece of the larger picture. Each person brings his own special background, beliefs, and ideas. Together, the pieces combine to form the culture of the United States!

Mosaics can be beautiful artwork. They can make even more beautiful countries.

Glossary

assimilation (uh-sih-muh-LAY-shun) The act of absorbing, or blending into, the customs of a group of people.

citizens (SIH-tih-zenz) People who were born in or have a right to live forever in a country or other community.

cultures (KUL-churz) The beliefs, practices, and arts of groups of people.

discrimination (dis-krih-muh-NAY-shun) Treating a person badly or unfairly just because he or she is different.

fluent (FLOO-ent) Being able to do something with ease, such as speak another language.

foreign (FOR-in) Outside one's own country.

identities (eye-DEN-tuh-teez) Who people are.

immigrants (IH-muh-grunts) People who move to a new country from another country.

mosaic (moh-ZAY-ik) A picture made by fitting together small pieces of stone, glass, or tile and pasting them in place.

natural-born citizens (NA-chuh-rul-BORN SIH-tih-zenz) People who are born US citizens. This includes people born in the United States and people born outside the United States with one or two parents who are US citizens.

naturalization (na-chuh-ruh-luh-ZAY-shun) The process of becoming a citizen.

population (pop-yoo-LAY-shun) A group of people living in the same area.

resources (REE-sawrs-ez) Useful things.

Index

Websites

Due to the changing nature of Internet links, PowerKids Press
has developed an online list of websites related to the subject
of this book. This site is updated regularly. Please use this link
to access the list:

www.powerkidslinks.com/mosa/first/